God Still Speaks

Whose Voice Are You Listening To?

S. D. Charlton

To order additional copies of this book, contact:
Xlibris Corporation
1-888-795-4274
www.Xlibris.com
Orders@Xlibris.com

In Loving Memory

To my hardworking and caring dad, Lloyd A. Charlton, who set the foundation for my siblings, me and others that hard work does pay off. Perseverance is essential to go forward, no matter the obstacles. You showed me what it means to be family oriented and how to think for myself and how to be creative. You took care of your large family no matter what. I watched your hard work and the endless giving of yourself. I just want you to know that I will always love you, and you will always have a place in my heart. We all miss you!

November 20, 1929 - February 16, 2006

To my loving and nurturing mother, Clara B. Charlton, who always had enough love for everyone. You made sure that your children were loved, fed, clothed, and educated. Not only did you see about your own children, but you always had a knack of seeing about and caring for other people and other people's children as well. You loved us when we were good and when we were not. You sacrificed and gave us the godly type of love that we needed. We never went hungry. How you took care of us all, I'll never know. Well, I know; it was the love of God that you had in your beautiful heart. Even when you were sick at the end, you still cared for others all the more. I will forever love you and think about you, Mom. We miss you dearly.

December 15, 1929 - January 25, 2005

Also in loving memory of my grandparents:
James Daniels, Annie Mae Swain and Otis Swain,
Edward Charlton and Elizabeth Charlton

Contents

I want to first give thanks and honor to God who is the head of my life. I dedicate this book back to the Lord. For without him, I truly would not have made it this far, and there would be no book. I can truly say that I am not my own; I belong entirely to him. In him I move, live, and have my being. Lord, you are truly the apple of my eye, and I love you. I thank you for loving me, when at times I didn't love or like myself. I am truly looking forward to that great day to see you face-to-face. What a joy that day will be!

Secondly, I dedicate this book to my parents, Lloyd A. Charlton and Clara B. Charlton, who are no longer with us on this earth. But we can still feel their presence nonetheless. I want to thank you, Mom and Dad, for your unconditional love. Thanks again for providing for my siblings and me. I don't know how you managed to keep us well fed and clothed, with all of those mouths you had to feed. Thank you for encouraging me through my rough times and even through my good times. Thanks for the morals and values that you have instilled in me.

Special Thanks

I want to give special thanks to all of my siblings: Sharon (Sharone), Janice (Janise), Deborah (Debbie), Carolyn (C. C.), Andrea (Andrie), James (Jimmy), Yolanda (Yolie), Leonard (Lenny), Olethia (Penny), Michael (Big Michael), Gary (Chew), and Lloyd Jr. (E.T.). You all have played a very special part in my life. I have nothing but warm childhood memories of the fun times we had playing together and even when we got into silly disagreements but came back together in love in no time flat. As of today, I thank God for you all. You are all so special to me, and I love each one of you dearly.

To Elder Edward Cook, even though you are no longer my pastor here in the great Buckeye state, I want you to know that through your teaching, preaching, guidance, rebuke, encouragement, and mentoring, you helped lay a solid foundation for me by the leading power of the Holy Ghost. I thank God for your great examples and ensamples as a man of God. I am sure that you are still empowering people even down in the Carolinas. May God continue to bless you and keep you! The best is yet to come.

Special tribute and thanks to the late Ollie C. West, who now has gone on to be with the Lord. Thank you for your unconditional love as my godmother.

To Marie Jones, who has edited a lot of my writings and critiqued them with a very honest eye, I appreciate you and thank you.

Thanks to all the others who had a part in the birth. God bless.

Preface

In our lives, we go from stage to stage, from test to test. And if we are not careful, we will miss a stage by running from what one might call woes or problems that life sometimes brings. Sometimes, life can be so painful until we want to find a way of escape through different means—for some it may be drugs, alcohol, sex, one's job, one's car, television, and even relationships (relationships can go into a category of its own)—instead of us allowing God to give us the strength to endure and come out as pure gold.

Oh, and let us not forget the tests of life that we go through. It is not all the time the devil is causing things to happen to us. It is oftentimes a test from God. The devil can do nothing without God's permission. And do know that a test does end. It's like being graded. If you flunk the test and get an F, you have to retake it until you pass it. Once you pass, you can go on the next test or phase. Believe me when I tell you I flunked plenty of times and, at times, still do. Then I find myself right back in that situation until I walk in total obedience. You know how we can be. We can be some hardheaded people at times.

So my purpose in writing this book is to encourage, to incite, to shake up, to wake up, to inspire, to trust God and take him at his word, and to let God have his way.

Strange enough, what got me on this road to writing was Black History Month back in 2003. While at work, I wrote a piece called "Stay Strong, My Brother, My Sister!" This was the first writing I ever wrote. You will see this particular one in this book.

I said to myself at the time, Lord, what is happening? Because my intention was to write something literally about Black History versus what you will be reading. However, the Lord led me in a different direction of unity for the body of Christ. I encourage you to read it for yourself. Then four years passed, and nothing else was written until December of 2007. From that point forward, God has not ceased to deal with me in such a manner as giving me revelations, inspirations, thoughts, ideas, solutions and warnings, and even encouragements concerning the things of his people and for this current world state, amongst other issues of life. He, our Lord Savior and Jesus Christ, has also dealt with me on my personal issues, triumphs and pain, perseverance, failures, victories and, most of all, salvation and holiness.

You would not believe me if I told you what I had to go through to even put this book together and get it published. The enemy fought me on every hand until at times I wanted to say "forget it." It really was a challenge leading up to the final stages. Of course, God prevailed.

So let us take this journey together as each page is read and meditated upon. Hopefully, this will be a life-changing experience to some, as well as enjoyment and empowerment to others. Let the Lord have his way as you read these inspired writings as a result of my own pains, heartaches, triumphs, victories, tests, and trials. And as you are reading this right now, God is yet shaping me, making me, and molding me. Our Christian walk is, indeed, a daily process until we see him face-to-face.

A City Paved in Gold

Oh what a great city with constant bright, illuminating lights. Oh my, what a city!

When you look around at the fortress of the city, what will you see? You will see many beautiful and wonderful things. Come and let's see.

Don't be surprised if you see foundation upon foundation of precious stones, like jasper, sapphire, chalcedony, emeralds, sardonyx, sardis, chrysolite, beryl, topaz, chrysoprase, jacinth, and oh my, do not forget the amethyst!

Have you ever wanted to walk on a street paved in goldlike clear glass? Well, get prepared with me to take a permanent journey to this great city, and you will see streets paved of pure gold like you have never seen. Please do leave all of your luggage behind. You will not need it where you are going.

Whatever else you do when you get there, feast your eyes on the dozens of pearly gates. These pearls are so breathtaking that it will put the pearls around your neck to shame!

Don't worry about trying to find a temple to worship in, because there is a great "Lamb" who is the temple himself. Oh, and the lights, do not even concern yourself about it. B'cause the glorified "Lamb" is the light himself.

Lastly, please do not forget to make preparations for this great life-changing trip! You do not want to miss it. Oh my, what a city. The city is New Jerusalem, with streets paved in pure gold.

May 8, 2008 5:53 a.m.

A Ripened Lily

My dearly beloved,

Your time has come to be plucked out of the field from the rest that have not yet yield.

You no longer have to worry about the labor that this world so oftentimes brings. For the toils and snares will be no more, for the time has come for a "ripened lily" to spring.

Your earthly body is now forever gone so that a "ripened lily" that you are can make it to God's holy throne. Done you are, you earthly vessel, from this life into heavenly fluorescence!

So the ones that are left behind don't have to mourn for the "ripened lily" that has now gone on. B'cause God has seen to it that it has a special place in the heavenly pearly gates for sure and that is forevermore...

"Ripened Lily," you are truly blessed b'cause our gracious Father has seen to it to pluck you from duress!

August 3, 2008 7:53 a.m.

9

All Glory and Honor Belong to Him

All glory and honor belong to him, for we know that he is the reason for things being into existence.

The stars, the moon, and the sun are all in tune with Our Majesty's Holy Word. The other awesome wonders and splendors were designed so that he would get all of the glory and honor that is definitely due to him.

Glory and honor belong to him; even the celestial and terrestrial bodies are in line with his word such as I am almost certain that you have heard.

The trees bow down to him, and the leaves clap their hands with total praise, for all glory and honor are for his glorious array!

All glory and honor belong to God for he created things as they should be, and he did not need any help from you and me to do it!

July 19, 2008 6:01 a.m.

Are Those Days Becoming Obsolete?

Where are the days when shouting in God's holy place of worship was supreme in that in it many victories were won, and the devil was for sure defeated? Have prim and properness claimed its fame and watered it down to nothing without shame?

Those days have been taken over by a generation and age of people of whom their holy ghost may need a little case of sharpening, along with some fine-tuning and grooming!

For Psalms 47:1 says for us to "Clap your hands, all ye people, shout unto God with the voice of triumph." Our God is wonderful and terrible, and he is greatly to be praised, which through him, many victories have been won and many souls have been saved.

We are to certainly bless his holy name. We need to bless him with a praise, with worship, a shout, and a testimony and a sho' nuff holy dance and with gladness and not just at a glance!

And whatever you do, please don't mistake a holy dance for a worldly dance that needs to quit it! That is why the question was raised, "Are those days becoming obsolete?" Or is it?

Our forefathers and the mighty cloud of witnesses had more power in one finger than we could ever imagine having in our whole body. The Holy Ghost was their claim to fame, and the power of God stated their claim forever without shame.

July 20, 2008 5:29 p.m.

Are You Enduring the Battle?

The battle is not given to the swift nor to the strong. So what is your excuse for not holding on?

Therefore, are you still enduring?

The battle is not given to the swift nor to the strong. So why are you whimpering and running scare as if you would dare?

Wherefore, are you still praying?

The battle is not given to the swift nor to the strong. So how come you are trying to fight it alone?

Therefore, are you still seeking and petitioning?

Since the battle is not given to the swift nor to the strong why are we trying to fight the battle with our own strength and might alone? Do know that the battle is not yours but it is the Lord's.

Therefore, are you still enduring? Are you still praying? Are you still seeking and petitioning?

No matter what, endure and run the race and know that your heavenly Father knows well what is at stake! So with that in mind, are you still enduring?

S. D. Charlton   December 30, 2007

Comfort in the Arms of Jesus

Tears seem to continue to flow like rivers of water that never end. All b'cause the heart, mind, and soul feel so heavy within.

There is comfort in the arms of Jesus, for he cares for you and knows what you are going through.

When that loved one is no longer around, and you sometimes feel so alone and like you cannot go on.

There is comfort in the arms of Jesus, for he said in his word that he will never leave you nor forsake you!

When the billows seem to blow and that loved one's presence feels oh so near and the heart breaks, so it seems without end.

God's comforting arms remain so dear, for he feels your pain too and beckons you to let him bear.

We may ask, how and when do the grief and pain stop? Only time, love, and God's comforting word will determine when that time is near. No matter what, your love and the missing of your loved one will ever remain ever so dear, and God's love and comfort will remain world without end.

For there is comfort in the arms of Jesus!

April 12, 2008   6:53 a.m.

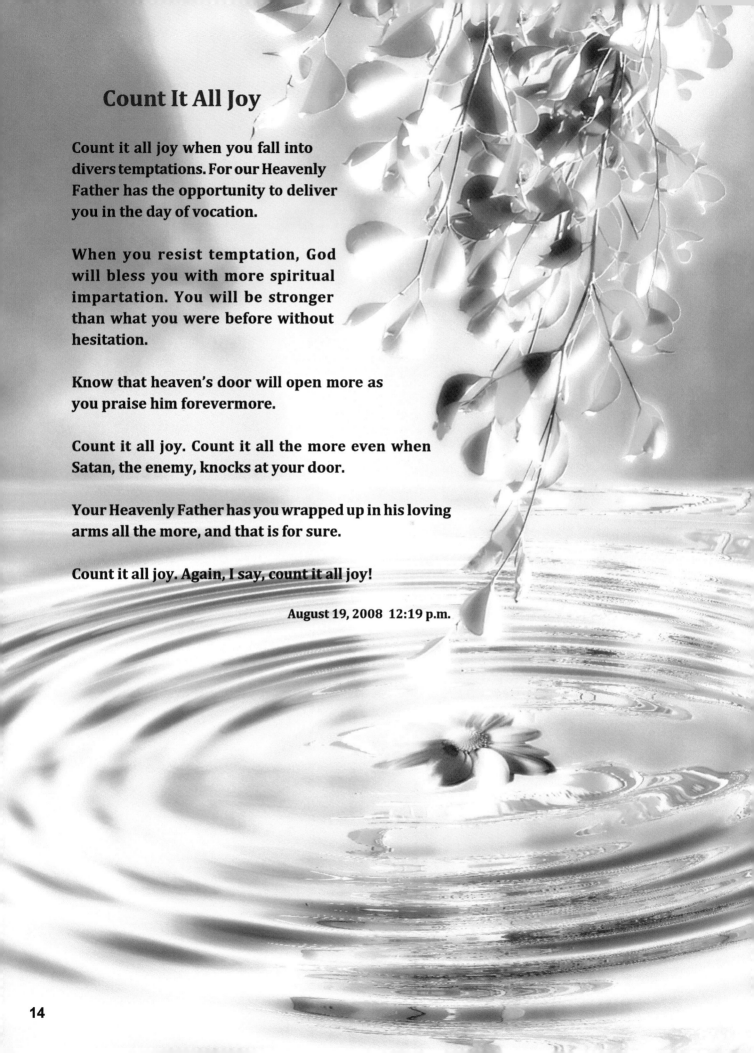

Count It All Joy

Count it all joy when you fall into
divers temptations. For our Heavenly
Father has the opportunity to deliver
you in the day of vocation.

When you resist temptation, God
will bless you with more spiritual
impartation. You will be stronger
than what you were before without
hesitation.

Know that heaven's door will open more as
you praise him forevermore.

Count it all joy. Count it all the more even when
Satan, the enemy, knocks at your door.

Your Heavenly Father has you wrapped up in his loving
arms all the more, and that is for sure.

Count it all joy. Again, I say, count it all joy!

August 19, 2008 12:19 p.m.

Get Filled with the Holy Ghost

You are living beneath your privileges because you are not filled with the Holy Ghost that strengthens you in your everyday living and issues.

It empowers. It enlightens, that is the Holy Ghost. So why won't you let him in to your life? B'cause know that he certainly would like!

A gentleman is he. He will not force himself on you or me.

Get filled with the Holy Ghost and let him rule your life so that misery and strife are not your way of life.

A comforter is he, and in his midst, he gives you the victory.

Get filled! Get filled! Get filled with the Holy Ghost because it is like having fire shut up in your bones that will not leave you alone!

August 8, 2008 6:00 a.m.

Glorified Body Is Coming for You!

Preparation is what we do. We do it thoroughly, and we do it through and through.

Make sure that it is a spiritual preparation in that your heart is pure. B'cause a glorified body is coming for you.

This earthly vessel will be no more. For it corrupts into nothing more than from ashes to ashes and dust to dust, back to earth from whence it cometh.

When that great day comes, your fleshly body will be no more. Your glorified body will take its place forever, and that's for sure.

God the Father, the Son, and the Holy Ghost eagerly await for you b'cause a glorified body is coming for you! Know that our Heavenly Father loves you through and through.

July 30, 2008 9:47 a.m.

God Don't Need No Coward Soldiers!

Many battles are fought, and many victories are won. Wherewith and how is this done? Does cowardice reign, or is boldness supreme? If God needed soldiers, what kind do you think they would be?

Of course, God would need boldness supreme, b'cause God don't need no coward soldiers to reign!

Why would not God need coward soldiers to reign? Would that soldier be subject to the devil's schemes, or would he or she stand for God's kingdom without hesitancy?

Battles are fought through much blood, sweat, and tears. Would that coward be able to take it without fear? (That is not fearing man but fearing God.)

When the devil increases with his schemes, will that soldier know that God's power still reigns supreme? And is he willing to pray without ceasing, no matter what fiery darts are thrown at him that seem to be ever-increasing?

Of course, that soldier better know that God is in control because God don't need coward soldiers running his show!

Are the battles we are talking about of a physical kind? No, of course not! We are talking about the ones where the weapons of our warfare are not carnal, but are mighty through God of pulling down of strongholds!

Therefore, we know that the battle is not ours, but it is the Lord's. Thus, we know that God don't need no coward soldiers to be in the way. B'cause God don't need no coward soldier ruining the race!

June 3, 2008 3:26 a.m.-4:26 a.m.

God Is . . .

When you look around you and see all of the beautiful things that God has made and created, all you can do is say God is . . .

Who would think to make trees green and skies blue, and who would think he created man to look like me and you!

The stars, the moon, the sun, and planets were created just for you and me so that we can separate the days from the nights and seasons and other things from what they should be. He created many things as well so that we can give him all the glory and honor that is due to him.

Thus, we know that God is . . . and then some. Why don't you just worship him?

When God said "peace be still," the raging sea obeyed and said that "we give in to Our Majesty!" When we call on the name of Jesus for our ailing health, and he simply says "you are now healed." We can truly say that God is . . .

God is all that we need him to be, all because of his amazing grace. He is so wonderful, and he is so great that he sacrificed his only Son so that we would have the choice to be saved from eternal damnation!

June 5, 2008 6:28 a.m.

God Is Still in the Saving Business!

We may say, what is happening to the miracles that used to be so prevalent?

Just take a look at me, and you will see a miracle that God saw fit to deliver from an eternal life of damnation.

He delivered me from my once sinful life that caused me much misery and strife.

So you see, God is still in the saving business, because he saw fit to save a sho' nuff wretch that once was pitiful and a wretched sinner.

God is still in the saving business! So please let him in, and he will deliver you from the "Son of Perdition" that wants you to very much burn in fiery hell! Lastly, for the enemy knows that for himself, all is not well.

August 10, 2008 10:06 p.m.

God Sees Your Tears!

Many times we wipe our eyes.
    We sometimes say to ourselves, "Lord, why? Why?"

Sorrows drench our souls from the problems and snares that seem to come at us unaware.
    But if we would only reach out to our Heavenly Father, who is always there, in it knowing that he does care.

For God sees your tears!
    He also knows about your secret fears.

Tears are precious to him as they are bottled up for a later heavenly reward.
    Meantime, the angels bring your tears to God to plead your cause so that you can move forward.

So bring all of your burdens to the Lord.
    And you tell him all about your troubles for sure.

God sees your tears! God sees your tears!

He knows about the secret things that life sometimes brings.
    Let him renew your heart so that your soul can now sing.

Trouble doesn't last always.
    Your private springtime is just at bay.

God sees your tears! God sees your tears!

Please wipe them away.
    Know that God will fix it for you all the day!

Remember again that trouble doesn't last always.
    Jesus's loving arms always are there to comfort you all throughout the day.

October 29, 2008 4:20 a.m.

God Will Wipe All Your Tears Away

When storms bellow, and the sea rages, and you do not quite know what to do, God will wipe all your tears away. Tears may come, and tears eventually cease, know that the Holy One's love shall ever increase.

In his word, he said he'll never leave you nor forsake you. He will hold on to you when the heart feels even sometimes blue, and you do not even have a clue what it is that is happening to you.

When life sends you blows and there is no one there to turn to, know that you have God's word to hold to very dear. For in his word, he said to cast all of your cares to him, for he cares for you, and he knows what you are going through.

No matter what, trust the Lord with all of your heart, mind, body, and soul.

Not only will he wipe all of your tears away, but he will bottle them up for a later heavenly stay!

Tears are precious to him, we know, for the Bible tells us so. Even through these tears, you can still find peace within, b'cause he will wipe them away when you come to him.

Sometimes tears are a necessary thing to cleanse the heart, mind, and soul that feels oh so heavy within. After the cleansing, you can surely find redemption without the seemingly constant whimpering.

So finally, my brother, my sister, let the tears flow, b'cause eventually they will cease to be forever for sure. For we know that he'll wipe all of your tears away, without a doubt, with his heavenly host aboard aiding and abetting all the way forevermore!

December 31, 2007 11:25 a.m

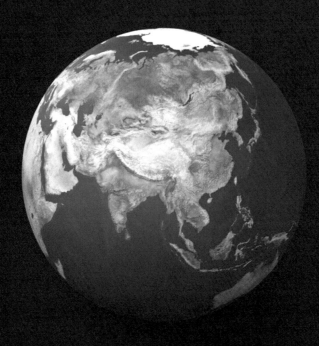

Has the World Crept in the Church?

Has the world crept into the church? When you look around, you cannot distinguish the world from the church. Take another look and tell me, what do you see? You may see shorts so short that it will make you blink in disbelief!

Saints of God, saints of God, what is going on? Are you trying to imitate the world's ways and quirks so they will favor your place of worship? How do you expect to draw the world by the indwelling of the Holy Spirit if you are knowingly or unknowingly imitating them!

Get it together, and get it together now, for time is too short to fool around. Again, has the world crept into the church? Yes, it has. You cannot tell that it has because you are so busy imitating them yourself.

One may say times have changed in that nothing stays the same. I am here to tell you that it is not true, for if you truly seek him, the Holy Ghost will bring you into all truths in that his word still remains as it is proclaimed.

Is there still healing, deliverance, and repentance like it used to be, or has the world's ways and spirit crept in to delay what was ordained to be?

Creep out, you worldly spirit, for God's predestined plan for redemption and salvation is still in force whether you like it or not! Church, Church, get it together, because he is coming back for a church without spot, wrinkle, or blemish.

May 11, 2008 7:57 a.m.

Humble Yourself

Pray and seek the Almighty's face so that you are in tune with what is rightfully yours in order to stay in his holy race!

Stay there until you hear from him. So that you know your praying was not done just on a whim.

But first you must humble yourself before the ""Alpha and the Omega" and " the Great I am" so that your prayers are not done in vain, because for sure, that would be a shame.

Humble yourself! Humble yourself! Humble yourself, and don't you dare put God on a shelf.

For he is real, and he is the one that will keep you from burning hell!

August 19, 2008 10:34 a.m.

I Got a Right to Praise Him!

Don't worry about why I am shouting and dancing before the Lord. You just simply don't know why I'm getting my praise on.

I got a right to praise him. I got a right to praise him.

After all I've been through, who are you to say what I should do?

I've been lied on, mistreated, and called everything that can't be repeated. So now you know that the devil is defeated!

I got a right to praise him! I got a right to praise him!

August 19, 2008 10:52 a.m.

If I Had Two Wings, Where Would I Go?

With two wings, one can fly north, and one can fly south. One can also fly east, and one can fly west. Two wings can take you where one wants to be!

But really and truly, with two wings, where would you go? Would you soar to the seven seas, or would you try to reach heaven at its highest peak?

If I had two wings, I would go where the mighty clouds of witnesses are looking down at me like Moses, David, and Abraham shouting, "Run, run the race, my sister, with continuity, for we are cheering you on, knowing that you have the victory!" Yes, that is where I want to fly and be with my brothers that are already there in eternity.

Most of all, I would want to fly where Jesus is to see him face-to-face. And to hear him say, "Well done, thy good and faithful servant, you can now rest in me, knowing that you made it to that great day of heavenly eternity."

May 6, 2008 12:22 p.m.

In the Last Days

Look around and see the signs of the times. You don't have to look too far. Just take a look at what surrounds you immediately.

For we know that in the last days, there will be many wars and rumors of wars. Nation shall rise against nation. Hearts are fainting because of fear, which lets you know that the time is near!

Yes, indeed, are we living in the last days. So get ready and prepare yourself so that you do not perish in it by getting caught unaware.

In the last days, man's heart is waxing colder and colder. He doesn't seem to care about the man who has a burden. He has become a lover of himself in that he only cares about what pleases him.

Get ready! Get ready before it's too late, because God's judgment day is nearer at the gate than you could ever anticipate. For we are living in the last days. This is just making it plain.

July 18, 2008 6:21 a.m.

In the Stillness of the Night

In the stillness of the night, the peace and quiet make it allright. The voices of man have ceased as God's holy voice has increased.

The darkened haze has covered the earlier sunrays with haloed lights that illuminate the shaded skies. Thank God for a quiet night that enables me to get more spiritual insight on the things that were, and the things that are, and the things which may come into being. In this I give thanks to God for everything.

The stillness of God's voice runs like many rivers of water to my soul. My heart clings to it like never before. It comforts me and gives me blessed assurance.

God is trying to tell his people something, that is why in the stillness of the night, his voice beckons with much faithful delight!

July 26, 2008 9:58 a.m.

Intercessors from God

Who is calling on the name of the Lord both day and night on behalf of people, things, and situations?

Who stays on bended knees in addition to lying prostrate before the Lord at wee hours of the morning? Who cries out to the Lord so that situations and adverse things can be turned around into a shouting victory?

They are called intercessors, prayer warriors, watchmen, and blood pleaders! Boldness is their name and God-seeking is their flame.

Intercessors from God labor in prayer to annihilate the devil's schemes and plans. They call out by faith many strongholds, hindering spirits or anything that comes against God's kingdom and for lost souls who need to come to Jesus.

They do this by binding and loosing so that the adversary can't escape its total damnation! This is done so that he, our Lord and Savior Jesus Christ, can block the devil from trying to destroy his kingdom by the devil's cowardly ways as he thinks he pleases.

Intercessors from God, intercessors from God, please continue to pray, labor, fast and meditate, and march on, for Jesus's second coming is just right around the corner!

July 24, 2008 11:29 a.m.

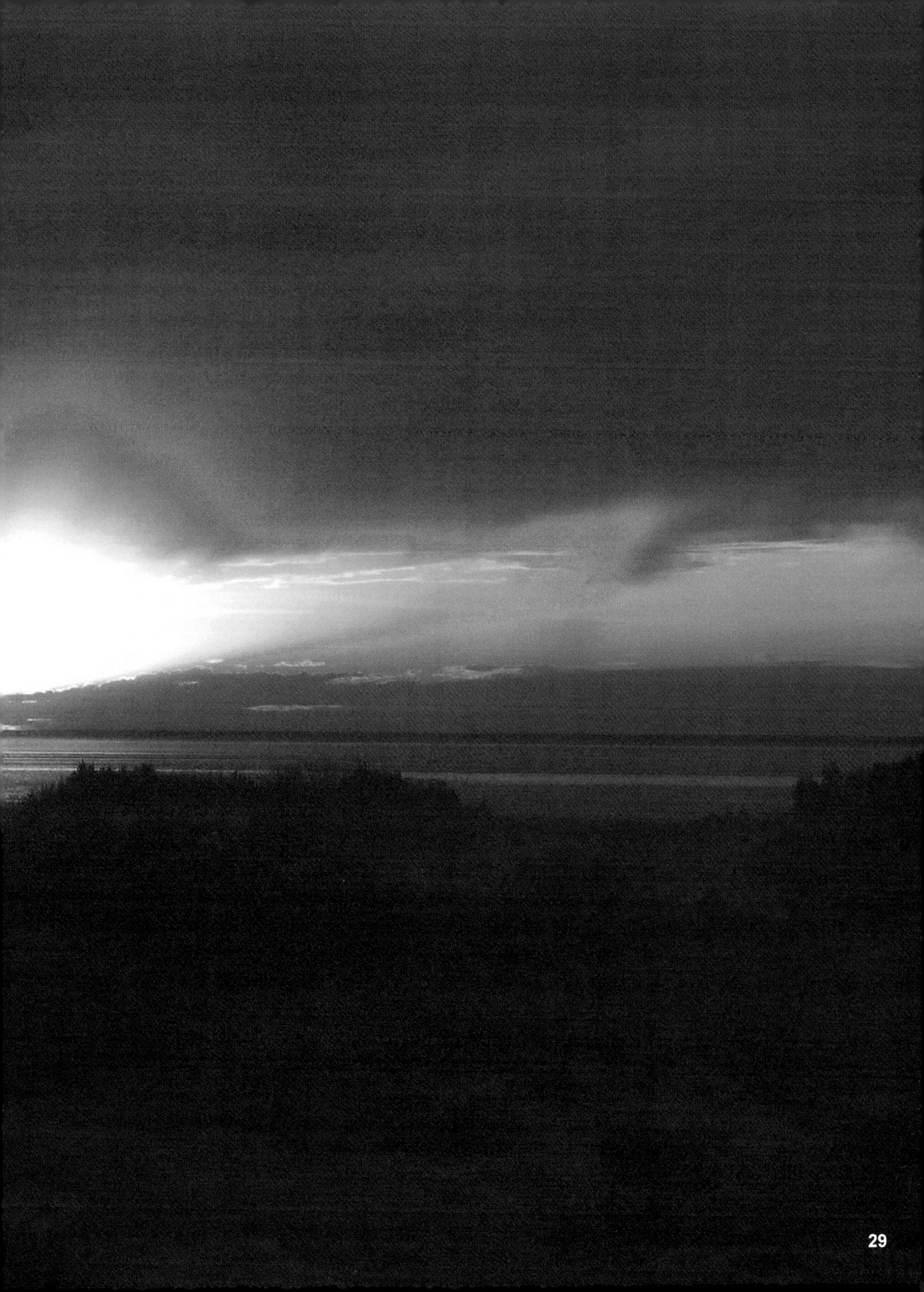

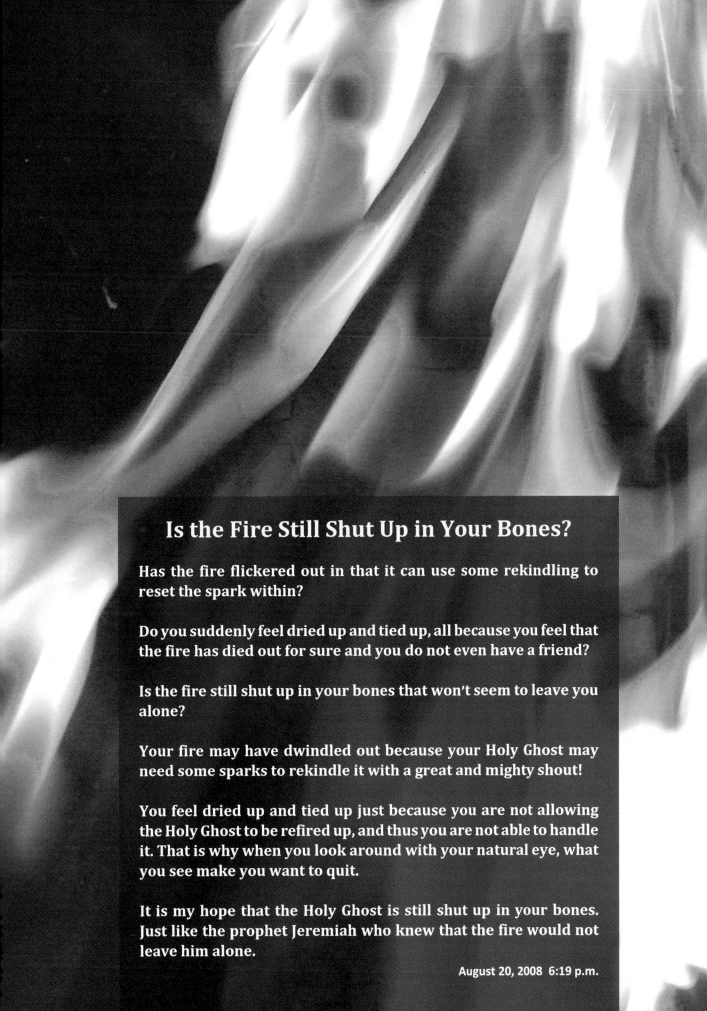

Is the Fire Still Shut Up in Your Bones?

Has the fire flickered out in that it can use some rekindling to reset the spark within?

Do you suddenly feel dried up and tied up, all because you feel that the fire has died out for sure and you do not even have a friend?

Is the fire still shut up in your bones that won't seem to leave you alone?

Your fire may have dwindled out because your Holy Ghost may need some sparks to rekindle it with a great and mighty shout!

You feel dried up and tied up just because you are not allowing the Holy Ghost to be refired up, and thus you are not able to handle it. That is why when you look around with your natural eye, what you see make you want to quit.

It is my hope that the Holy Ghost is still shut up in your bones. Just like the prophet Jeremiah who knew that the fire would not leave him alone.

August 20, 2008 6:19 p.m.

It's Okay to Be Single and Free!

Single women and men of God, hold your head up and don't you dare look down. For our Heavenly Father has you in this present state for his awesome glory and power and heavenly array.

Marriage is great, and holy matrimony is sacred and pure. But please don't make a mistake in thinking that being single is full of loneliness and blues.

Please take advantage of this precious state that God has set apart for his use. Just think of the great works you can do without having to worry or be concerned about, maybe hearing, "Honey, I'm home! Where is my home-cooked food?" or "Sugar, did you fix that plumbing so that the toilet will stop running?"

God knows when or if that precious union will take place. So it is okay to be single and free, knowing that God still gives singles sustaining grace along with the awesome victory in being content in your current state.

Finally, whatever you do, please do not think of being single as being an awful thing. Instead, rise up and stand up knowing by shouting, "It is okay to be single and free to carry out God's will with ease and grace!"

August 20, 2008 9:07 p.m.

Let Him Renew Your Strength

Let him anoint you so that his power is released into being. Let him appoint you into what he wants you to be!

So wait upon the Lord and let him renew your strength. When that is done, your sho' nuff victory is what it is.

Your strength comes from within. It comes from the one who knows all about it to no end.

Let him renew your strength so that you become not weary in your well doing. Keep the faith and keep on pursuing.

Let him renew your strength! Let him renew your strength, for in it, you are able to go through all things without a flinch!

August 10, 2008 10:10 a.m.

Let Him Take You Beyond the Veil

Do you want to go with me to a place that is
so powerful until flesh can't handle it?

This is a place where the Shechinah glory rests, rules,
and abides. Believe me, once you enter into God's
presence beyond the veil, then you know that it is no
lie.

So let him take you beyond the veil. Let him take you
beyond the veil in it you know that you certainly have
dwelled.

God wants to do a new thing in you.
Please don't worry about what you need to do.

All you have to do is to let yourself go.
Allow God's Holy Spirit to flow.

In his mighty presence, there is peace,
love, and joy. Just the thought of it should make
you want to weep with fervent joy.

When you come out, you won't be the same.
Your countenance should have a fluorescent gleam.

So let him take you beyond the veil.
Allow your heart to break so that
He can mend it and allow you to prevail!

                    August 19, 2008 10:39 a.m.

Let Him Work It Out

While we are trying to figure it out, God has got it already worked out. This alone should make you want to shout!

Jesus will fix it for you. Please just have faith and allow him to turn it around for your good and let him work it out through and through.

Let him work it out. Let him work it out.

And whatever you do, don't you doubt. So stop worrying about how it looks, because before you know it, Jesus will have moved on your behalf and worked it out before you can even pout.

Just keep the faith. Continue to run this holy race.

Let him work it out. Let him work it out.

August 19, 2008 12:29 p.m.
Photo taken by "ABCDZ200" (Pen name)

Let Your Worship Be True

Let your worship be true and let it be right. B'cause this is the only way to enter into his presence without your own strength and might.

Go before God's throne just knowing who he is. Lie before the Master's feet and let your worship be for real.

For starters, please pray for a pure heart so that your spirit will be in tune to the One that beckons you from above. Let his spirit woo you and let it handle you as gentle as a dove.

Let your worship be true by recognizing who he is and seeking his face world without end. Allow the Lord to cleanse you within.

Let it be true! Let it be true b'cause our Heavenly Father wants to do a new thing in you.

August 10, 2008 9:58 p.m.

Lie at the Masters Feet

Why don't you lie at the Master's feet? Bring your solemn tears along with a reverent fear.

Make sure that you bring humility, obedience, and the likes and all. So your sharp spiritual ear, soul, body, and mind will be boldly entwined withal.

That is entwined with the Master, who beckons for us to lie at his feet. In it, he'll give you much spiritual food and plenty to eat.

Lie at the Master's feet! Lie at the Master's feet. Stay there until you are endued with being meek but not spiritually weak.

August 19, 2008 10:45 a.m.

My Redeemer

My Redeemer lives in me and carries me all the day long. My Redeemer enables me to move, live, and have my being so that he can have his way withal.

Redemption comes here, and redemption is now. What are you waiting for? Grab on to him now and don't you doubt. He comes to save and to give you grace, so please do not hesitate.

My Redeemer restores the peace within when I didn't think I even had a friend to share things that I so often held within. Salvation is now, and it is waiting for you with opened arms. He is waiting to share his grace and mercy so that you will not dare be without.

Who made the sun, moon, and the stars? Who made it rain when the grass, trees, and flowers were crying within to be watered so that renewal can take place without flinching?

My Redeemer is his name. He had a claim to fame before the world even knew his name.

June 6, 2008 10:15 a.m.

Never Seen the Righteous Forsaken

Saints of God who have the Holy One entrenched in their hearts. Know that our Heavenly Father has you wrapped in his loving arms.

I have never seen the righteous forsaken. Nor have I seen any of God's seed begging bread.

So please stop worrying where you are going to get your next your meal. Know that through your Heavenly Father, you have the real deal.

Again, I have never seen the righteous forsaken. I repeat, I've never seen the righteous forsaken.

Stop your crying, because God will keep you from dying. And stop the constant whining by trusting God to come through with his perfect timing.

August 19, 2008 12:17 p.m.

Preparation for This Journey

Leave your luggage. Forsake your bags and leave all of your worldly possessions behind. For the time is near and the time is short. Make preparations to dwell eternally with the Heavenly Host.

Get your tickets and buy them now. For a time will come when you will not be able to purchase them at all!

Purify your heart and cleanse it please. Make sure that you repent on bended knees. Are you running late, or are you ready for a prepared everlasting journey that will not wait?

Preparation for this journey should not be too hard! All you have to do is to humble yourself before the "Great I Am" and the "Almighty God" and repent to him and say, "Lord, please forgive me. I have fallen short from your grace. I believe that you died and rose again for my sins for this very day."

Lastly, do not think that this earthly vessel is going to heaven above, but know that it will be a glorified one. For the preparation for this journey is mapped out for us with every detail already in place!

May 8, 2008 5:45 a.m.

Repent Ye! Repent Ye!

Come on everybody. Let's get it together, for the kingdom of heaven is at hand in that, we better. Get it right! Get it right! For we know not the day nor the hour when he is coming.

Repent ye! Repent ye, everyone, and get it right, for we know not when and we know not the time. Rest assured that he is coming like a thief in the night!

Are you right with God? Are you right with God? Are you sanctified, Holy Ghost-filled and fire-baptized? And are you praying with all of your might?

Come on and go with me to a place where your spirit will truly be blessed! Do not hesitate, for it might be everlastingly too late lest you repent knowing that the kingdom of heaven is at stake.

Repent ye! Repent ye, you proclaimed child of God, for you don't want to be caught with your works undone. You sinner, you sinner, you better get it together, for Jesus is soon to come just like he said he would.

So please do not look back lest you want to turn into a pillar of salt like Lot's wife did when she beheld Sodom and Gomorrah's fate that led them to that dreadful day!

Are you on bended knees? Are you on bended knees, praying to the only one that can redeem? Are you sincere in that God will listen to you with a fervent ear?

Repent ye! Repent ye and don't turn back, if you do so, you'll surely miss out on your glorious crown in fact!

June 21, 2008 9:27 p.m.

Sanctify Yo'self

We go about our day thinking that we can live, move, and have our being through our own merit by living any old kind of way. But I come to tell that is not so because holiness is here to stay.

So please, whatever you do, sanctify Yo'self so that you can move and have your being through him without such as a whim.

What does all that mean about sanctifying Yo'self? It means that you need to set yo'self apart from the rest, and in that, he that is the Holy Ghost can raise you up so that you can be amongst the heavenly elect.

The next time you go about your day trying to fit in with the so-called in crowd that is the world per se. Know that it will not please your Heavenly Father, who knows the world's final judgment day!

Sanctify, sanctify, purify, purify Yo'self, for God is coming back for a church without spot, wrinkle, or blemish without any doubt. So please recognize and prepare yo'self because he is coming soon like he said he would; this should be something to shout about!

So get ready and sanctify Yo'self b'cause the people of the world will miss out on Jesus Christ's second coming! You do not want to be left behind with them whining and crying. Sanctify Yo'self, you lost, self-pleasing wretch; your eternal fate of damnation may start a humming.

June 18, 2008   11:41 p.m.

Seek the Old Landmark

We may say to ourselves. What is wrong with the churches today? Have things changed so much in the twenty-first century that holiness has taken second place?

Has the church become so contemporary and worldly that God's word has been sugar-coated for surely?

Yes, things have changed, and some of the people of God who have been called by his name have allowed Satan to come in and have his way. But do know this one thing though; God's word will remain the same as the Holy Bible states.

The church has become so contemporary that it has left God out of it. God's word is being sugar-coated to keep the church pews from becoming oh so vacant, and golden offering plates from being totally empty or forsaken?

Man pleasing has become the way until seeking the old landmark has got to be reclaimed.

We need more holiness. We need more holiness. We need more holiness to bring back the old landmark that has taken a backseat to some of the so-called contemporary things that have no power or substance to it or seedlings!

August 8, 2008 7:00 a.m.

Sorrow No Longer Drenches My Soul

My heart aches oh so within. For when I looked around, lo and behold, I had not even a friend.

Rejection reared its ugly head on every corner. It was done to make me think that I was not worth it.

However, my God came in and lifted up a standard so that I would know better. Know better not to believe all the lies the enemy tried to make me see.

For sorrow had drenched my soul. In that sometimes I thought I couldn't go on.

The loving God that I serve whispered in my ear and said, ""Run on, my darling child, and don't you fear"

He told me he loved me so like no human could. All because his love is unconditional, this is awesome within itself.

So now sorrow no longer drenches my soul because my Savior said to me, "Child, please be bold! And whatever you do, don't worry about what man says or thinks because I'm here with you through thick and thin, no matter what comes or goes!"

September 23, 2008 11:44 p.m.–11:57 p.m.

Stay Strong, My Brother, My Sister!

Be encouraged. Don't let the enemy see you sweat! Looking back on how our forefathers and our ancestors fought for their freedom and their rights, I can't help but think how many lives were sacrificed and how they pressed on no matter what. (Forefathers and ancestors apply to anyone who fought for what was right.) There is no excuse why we can't take a licking and keep on ticking. Not only that, we have God on our side if we allow him to be.

Instead of us fighting for what is right, we are fighting each other. My brothers and sisters, this should not be. This is not in reference to a physical war, but a spiritual one.""For we wrestle not against flesh and blood, but against principalities, against powers, against the rulers of the darkness of this world, against spiritual wickedness in high places" (Ephesians 6:12). We are giving the enemy too much space to come in to divide and conquer. We need to fight the good fight of faith together, not apart. We are not talking about Negroes, African Americans, coloreds, Nubians,[1] or whatever you wish to be called. We are talking about Jews, Gentiles, Christians, saints, friends, black, white, brown, or yellow. This applies to anyone who is willing to fight for what is right. Even if it means standing alone. Don't worry about the majority, because more often than not, the majority is wrong or too much of a coward to be counted. Again, stand and be strong and don t let the devil see you sweat. Let the Lord fight your battles.

Remember, we can do all things through Christ, which strengthens us. It is not how many times you fall that counts, but how many times you get back up again. Dust yourself off and keep on trying. A quitter never wins, and a winner never quits. Stay strong and hold your head up.

Finally, if you stand for nothing, you will fall for anything. Together we can and will make a difference in Christ!

February 19, 2003 3:00 p.m.

(A Black History Tribute)

---

1   *Nubian*: (1a) A member of one of the group of Negroid tribes that formed a powerful empire between Egypt and Ethiopia from the 6th to the 14th centuries. (1b) A native or inhabitant of Nubia (*Webster Dictionary*).

Stop Playing Church!

Stop going through the motions like your so-called dance don't need Holy Ghost-sharpening. If you don't cease from church-parading and ushering in worldly things, you give ground for your flesh to become supreme.

It is such a waste because God sees all and knows all of your going-through-the-motions charades. Be true to God and invite the Holy Ghost in so that your praise and worship will be of true essence and not a parade.

Stop playing church and lying to the Holy Ghost. For it grieves God to no end when your flesh sits at the head.

Repent before God and let him have his way so your playing church can be dissipated! Then you can have true praise.

August 8, 2008 6:57 a.m.

The Abuse of Power

Preacher men, teacher men, who do you think that you are fooling? God has granted and anointed you with this special gift, but please do not make a mistake by thinking that you can abuse it!

Get it together, men and women of God. Please don't think that you can go around with "the abuse of power wrapped around your neck." For God sees all and knows all even when you think that no one else can catch it.

So don't think that you can hide in the corner when you're doing wrong. For my God sits high and sits low and still reigns supreme on his heavenly throne!

Repent before the Almighty God. Seek to do your first work over so that accountability with him won't be overwhelming and overloaded.

Don't scatter the sheep b'cause they are not yours; furthermore, they were never yours to even keep. For the Holy One has you as the undershepherd over them to lead and guide them in the right direction so that their soul shall keep until that great day of reckoning.

The abuse of power seems to be happening more and more these days. Just make sure that you're not the one caught in this fatal state. And thank God for those who are still faithful and are still in God's holy race.

Finally, the abuse of power must go away so that God's work may go forth without further delay!

July 18, 2008 6:27 a.m.

The Fiery Skies

Who made the fiery skies? Who blessed us where we can look at them and say to ourselves with glorious cries, "Oh my, my"?

God strong mighty in battle is his name. Taking the foolish things of this world to confound the wise is his flame!

The fiery skies denote his decorative glory. If you take the time to view them, they will tell you a story.

If you ever want to see something beautiful and amazing, just take a look at God's fiery skies to view as they are certainly ablazing!

October 24, 2008 10:14 a.m.

Photo taken by Steven P. Williams
October 2008
Taken in Gatlinburg, Tennessee

The World Is Trying to Imitate the real thing?

Is the world trying to imitate the real thing all because the world wants the true power and strength that it brings?

Unless you repent and do it now, your chance to ask the Savior into your life might be the thing of the past. For know that the things of the world do not last.

World, World, who do you think you are fooling? Just because you use our Savior's name, it does not mean that you are truly! Satan uses the world to imitate and mimic God's ways, but if you are truly in tune with God's Holy Spirit, you would know that it is just a fake!

People of the world, stop trying to mimic God's people through your song and dance, for when Lucifer was thrown out of heaven, as so, he lost his godly stance.

The only way to become one with the most high is to turn away from your wicked ways. Then you may now accept him as Lord and Savior, Jesus Christ, for he died that you may have eternal life today!

June 24, 2008 8:12 a.m.

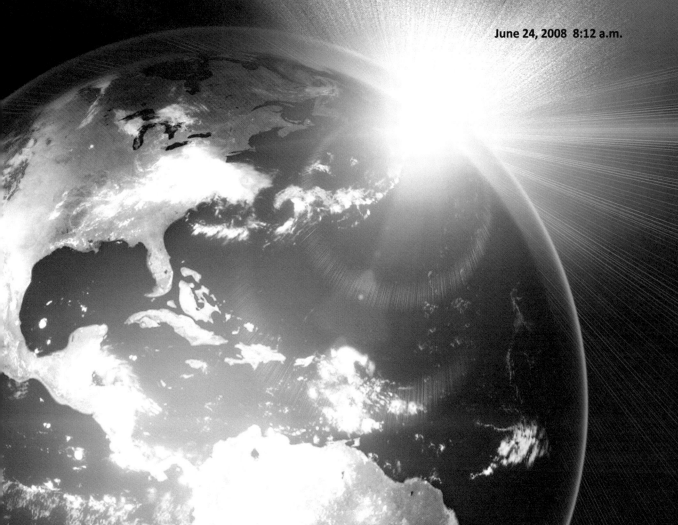

They Smile in My Face

They smile in my face with teeth oh so bright and white, but behind that smile is a case of deadly lethal injection. Encouragement is what they do with evil perfection so they choose!

Watch out for the smiling mask whose task is to devour you with their evil presence and to get you at last with their ever-deceitful schemes that try to scream.

Thank God for Jesus, for with him there is no lack. For no matter what arrows are thrown my way, he enables them to be hurled right back at them!

They smile in my face! All because they want to destroy me with their words in order to take my place. Thank God for being my deliverer and my constant stay. I thank you, God, for everything!

July 24, 2008 6:05 a.m.

This World Is Not My Home

Sometimes we find ourselves getting caught up in the world affairs. As we can, of course, lose foresight on the great afterlife that God has so graciously prepared.

For I know that this world is not my home. I am just a pilgrim passing through.

I just can't feel at home anymore. My life here is just a foretaste of the glory to come.

So don't get too comfortable in this current world per se. B'cause the world to come is much, much better than one can ever ask or think!

This world is not my home. And I do not permanently belong!

August 8, 2008 5:34 a.m.

Wait On the Lord

Trials may come, and trials may go. Just know that God is working it out for your good no matter what.

Wait on the Lord and be of good courage and allow him to strengthen your heart. In waiting, you have a chance for a brand-new start.

Begin to praise him. Begin to do a holy wave for him. For in his own time, he'll bring you out, and there is no doubt.

Don't you dare worry about how it looks. Just let go and let God and allow your spirit to be hooked!

Wait on the Lord. Wait on the Lord. Wait on the Lord.

And whatever you do, let him strengthen your heart! God Almighty will renew your mind with a fresh start.

Wait! Wait! He'll sho' nuff bring you out!

Wait, I say, on the Lord.

August 19, 2008 12:21 p.m.

Wake Up, Sleeping America!

Look around you, and what do you see? Do you see destruction right at your door that makes you want to flee?

Repent, you materialistic nation. Seek the God of your forefathers who paved the way for you so that all of their getting and doing was not done in vain for you.

America, regroup and recognize where your priorities should be. Once you do, you will have the right now and eternal victory.

So wake up, sleeping America, from your deepened trance. Realize that the God of your forefathers wants to give you a second chance!

September 16, 2008 8:50 a.m.

Wake Up, Sleeping Beauty

Wake up, Sleeping Beauty, from your state of contentment. Wasn't the destruction of the Twin Towers on 9/11 enough to bring you to repentance?

You may say, Repentance from what? From your wayward ways that is causing your current failing and fatal state!

Was it not enough to cause you to repent from your idolatry ways that have been keeping you from Jesus from day to day?

Wake up, America, before more destruction cometh at your door. Get down on bended knees and confess so that your eternal life won't be out of sorts.

Wake up, Sleeping Beauty, and make your call and election sure. So that you can make it through heaven's door forevermore!

September 18, 2008 10:25 a.m.

Was Not Fit to Live

My life was nothing until you came into my life at the time when I was not fit to live nor was I fit to die. What great timing because I was saying to myself at that time, "Oh Lord, my, why, why am I still alive!"

What a great and mighty God that we serve, who saved me and gave me eternal life when I was not deserving of it. You transformed me so that I would not conform to the world in which I was once so much a part of as I saw fit.

So now I can boldly tell others that even though you are not fit to live nor fit to die, allow Jesus Christ to come into your life. God's grace and mercy give us a chance to be shaped and molded to the image of him!

Finally, thanks be to God, I am being shaped and molded for heaven. So those who are not saved, do it now, for you do not want your soul to be doomed for that great day of reckoning.

June 5, 2008 8:26 a.m.

What About War?

As the word states as it is appointed unto men once to die.
What follows is judgment, and that is no lie.

What about war? Has it not killed many innocent ones in scores?

Bear in mind that there is nothing wrong with fighting for one's country in its season. At this time, is fighting now the right reason?

The Bible says that there is a time of war and a time of peace. So at this given time, is this the time to cease?

For we know God has set certain things in place. However, is now the time for our fellow man, our fellow soldiers, and our country to continually fight in the seemingly rat race?

What about war? Should we not listen to the voice of the one that has the keys to heaven and hell forevermore?

For if you listen to our Heavenly Father's voice, we the country, the people, the saints, and the world will repent and do our first works over again. That is why repentance is needed by all to forsake so much sin.

So what about war? Should the fight go on and on as innocent bodies continue to get washed ashore?

July 18, 2009
6:30 a.m.

In loving memory of Lloyd A. Charlton Sr.
November 20, 1929- February 16, 2006

What Will Demons Do?

We go around saying, "Oh, demons are not real all because you are not praying for the spirit of discernment"; therefore, the thought may seem quite surreal. Wake up, everybody, and know that smell of sulfur is the odor of the demons that will leave you gagging and gawking.

So the question was asked, what will demons do? I am here to tell you that they will run you out of your shoes if you do not have a clue. It is best that you get prayed up, oiled up, and worded up and fasted up so that one day, they won't jump or sneak upon you!

The Father has given us the shield of protection that is his precious Holy Ghost that is there to keep you! Oh, and do get discernment, and you better get it now so that they won't catch you off guard without having your shield and armor on.

Stop saying you wonder where they are housed. But simply know that if you allow them, they will get into or on human bodies just like yours and mine.

Again, what will demons do? They will have you acting ugly and acting like a fool without you really trying to.

They'll have you doing things that you normally would not do or say. That is why God's comforter, which is the Holy Ghost, is a protector through and through, and it is here to stay!

June 23, 2008 11:13 p.m.

You Gotta Have Faith!

Mountains may seem high. The valleys at times are too low. Forests seem so deep in that if you want to see the other side, you cannot just take a mere peek.

Since these obstacles seem so great, why don't you just have faith! Faith in God does wonders, for it has healed the sick and raised the dead. So I'm simply telling you that you gotta have faith!

Faith is not sight. It is trust and belief in the things that you simply cannot see. The clincher is to keep your hand in the Master's hand, knowing without a shadow of a doubt that he'll bring you out with a mighty shouting victory.

You gotta have faith, for it moves God to no end. It shows that you truly trust in him.

You gotta have faith and don't you give up! God's reinforcement is just at the door.

Thus, don't wait until the battle is over, shout the victory right now. For you simply gotta have faith and again shout out loud!

You gotta have faith! You gotta have faith!

July 17, 2008 6:14 a.m.

You Must Be Born Again!

You have been bought with a price. You have a choice to choose life.

Choose life by accepting Jesus Christ, who died a long time ago so that sin would not have dominion. Thus, your life will not be so full of woes and ungodly whimpering!

It does not necessarily mean when you come to Jesus, your life will be full of roses. Just simply read God's Word about the life of Moses.

So make a choice by listening to the inner voice of God, who beckons you to come. If you don't listen to that inner voice, your sinful life to it will you continue to succumb.

Come to him, because you must be born again. Repent and give your life over to him; you must be born again!

Please listen to witnesses who beckon you to abort your sins. Become regenerated and allow him in.

You must be born again! You must be born again!

You must be born again by acknowledging your sin. Also, by acknowledging that the Holy One died and rose again!

You must be born again! Don't wait too late to repent of your sin!

For salvation is the only way that you will make it in. Simply put, you must be born again.

August 20, 2008 9:07 a.m.

Picture of Ellie (Catherine Reeves)
Daughter of John and Lindsey Reeves

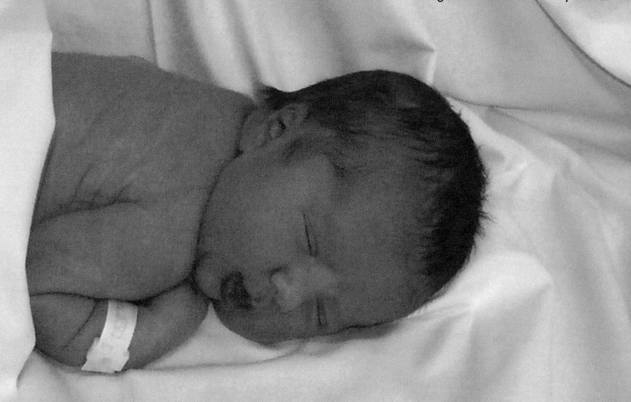

To Mother Hargrove: 1-18-15
(Sunday)

Blessings, glory and honor I speak to you. I speak great + mighty blessings and healing unto you.

Continue to strive and press toward the mark which is a higher calling of Christ Jesus!

Much Love,
Elder Sandra D Charlton